Shayla & Friends

A True Story of Rescue, Faith, and Finding Home

Barchelle Bolger Wathen

Love will find you
When you need it most.
When you're scared
Listen with your soul,
Hear Love call you forth
Even across the oceans.

By Barchelle (Chelly) Bolger Wathen

Dedication

This story is dedicated to God (the original Author), and to the inspiration of the Roman Korniyko family, Mykola Yuhimenko, and the children of OTCHIY DIM (Father's House), a Christian orphanage in Ukraine. And their compassionate supporters like Bruce and Anne Elliott, who helped Shayla find her forever home in America.

I remember the animals lost or abandoned in Ukraine's war turmoil—especially Nala of Father's House—gone but never forgotten.

And to every rescue dog and sanctuary, especially Blackhat Humane Society and Dogtree Pines Senior Dog Sanctuary, who blessed our lives with your friendship. Blackhat gave us more than a dog; their compassion saved Tayen and brought him home to complete our family

Contents

Introduction

Father's House (Otchiy Dim) home

*"**Have I not** commanded you? Be strong and courageous. Do not be afraid; do not be discouraged, for the Lord your God will be with you wherever you go."* — Joshua 1:9 (New International Version)

Life requires courage—from people and from animals. Long before Shayla, a stray puppy with no hope, ever found a kind hand or crossed the ocean to America, God was already giving her strength and courage to survive freezing winters and boiling summers, extreme hunger, and loneliness.

In Ukraine, the Christian orphanage Otchiy Dim (aka Father's House) stands as a sanctuary of peace and love. There, abandoned children, and animals, are welcomed, protected, and cherished as precious lives. Roman Korniyko, along with his wife and daughters, Anastasia and Alina, devoted their lives to building this refuge.

Through seasons of scarcity, political unrest, and uncertainty, Roman courageously followed God's direction, stating, "true happiness comes in following God's path of love."

This is not only the true story of Shayla, a dog rescued from Ukraine, it is the story of how God works through unlikely friendships, second chances, and faithful obedience. It is the story of how He weaves together hurting children, rescue dogs, distant nations, and broken hearts into a tapestry of hope and love.

The chapters that follow share my journey, my dogs, and the treasured true stories that became the foundation for the *Shayla & Friends* and *Shayla's Adventure* series. Like a worship song that kept echoing in my heart, I was reminded how God is with us in every detail of our lives, even the tough moments.

Wherever your own journey leads, I hope you find the courage to take the next step—even when the path feels uncertain.

Chapter One
Come Join the Journey

Shayla's journey - at the crossroads

***Who are you**, really?* I suspect you may be a fellow dog lover, Ukraine supporter, or an adventurer at heart – in pursuit of a cause that ignites your passion?

Or perhaps you are someone who has loved deeply, lost painfully, and wondered how all the pieces of your life will ever fit together.

Wherever you find yourself, I invite you to come along on this journey.

At first glance, this may seem like the story of a rescue dog named Shayla. And it is. But looking back, I can see how God was quietly shaping my heart in those ordinary days. Seeds planted through my life culminated in who I finally became, each step leading to the next in His plan across time. It is a story about rescuing and being rescued. About discovering that sometimes the ones we think we are rescuing are, in truth, rescuing us.

Shayla's life began on the cold streets of Ukraine, a lonely stray pup, just trying to survive. My life began oceans away in San Diego, California, long before I ever heard of a country called Ukraine, and long before I knew that a stray dog would one day come into my life in a way only God could have arranged. But every meaningful journey begins long before we recognize it.

For me, the journey began with dogs.

I grew up in a suburban neighborhood in San Diego with two older brothers, and parents who had roots in the farmlands of Minnesota. Though I did not grow up on a rural farm, our home was never without at least one dog and a couple of cats. My first companions as a young child were our pets. Bokie the beagle, Fritz (a police officer's pet shepherd), and Riska, our gentle Elk-Kee (Norwegian elkhound/keeshond mix). Each brought their own kind of magic. Even our cats, rescued Siamese and a white matriarch with her kittens, found their way into our hearts. But it was the dogs who especially taught me unconditional love. They were my companions when my brothers left for college and I felt like an only child. Animals were never "just pets." They were always family.

As a shy, awkward junior high schooler, in braces, and the daughter of a disciplinarian substitute teacher, I found solace in a group of six close friends known as the "good kids" who focused on good grades), and also in the steady companionship of my dogs.

My dogs did not measure worth by popularity or performance. They did not care whether I was athletic, confident, or socially polished. They greeted me the same way every day—tail wagging, eyes bright, heart open, my quiet refuge. They couldn't fix my problems or offer witty advice. They simply listened without judgment, laid by my side, head in my lap, not saying a word.

Looking back, I see how God was shaping my heart to love dogs in those ordinary days.

How do you embark on a journey of self-discovery? Not with a map, but with a mirror.

I've often wondered how many of us walk through childhood unaware of the seeds God is planting for our future. Who has He placed in your life to shape you, challenge you, and teach you?

I believe those key characters in our lives are there by God's intentional design, to shape who we become. Over the years, I have been blessed to be a sister (little and big), niece, aunt, paralegal, supervisor, ombudsman, student, teacher, author, hiker, and adventurer (love those ziplines), just to name a few. But the roles that have most deeply touched my heart are wife, daughter, friend, Christian, and dog mom.

Each role added a layer to my understanding of compassion and responsibility, helping me discover my passions and life purpose. Each relationship led me, step by step along what my friend Roman called "God's path of love."

Growing up, I did not know that loss would visit my life. That grief would carve spaces in my heart I could not fill on my own. That faith would deepen not in comfort, but in uncertainty.

And I certainly did not know that across an ocean, in a country I had never heard of, a small stray puppy was beginning a story that would one day intertwine with mine.

Every journey has a beginning. Sometimes it looks ordinary. Sometimes it feels small. But in hindsight, we see the fingerprints of God even in the quietest seasons.

As you read, I invite you to reflect: *What roles have you played in your own life?* Examine those relationships that have stirred your spirit, and the dreams they awaken in your heart. *Have you been the rescuer, or the one who needed rescuing?*

Come join the journey.

Chapter Two
My Father's Light and Legacy

At the core of my story stands my wonderful father, Herbert Bolger. An ordinary looking man, but strong in stature and spirit. Strength has many forms, and his was the quiet kind. The kind that shows up, day after day, without fail.

As a child, I believed he could fix anything. As a teen and adult, I realized that included broken hearts.

I loved lighthouses from the first time my father took me to the Old Point Loma Lighthouse. I remember standing beside him, looking up at that steadfast tower, so tall against the blue sky, never imagining how that image would root itself in my heart. Only years later did I understand that my father had been my lighthouse all along.

He stood firm on a foundation of integrity and quiet strength, steadily weathering every storm that swept across our lives. My refuge. When the waters felt uncertain, he offered calm, sage words that guided me back to solid ground. My father was both the lighthouse and the keeper—faithful, humble, and always shining for everyone in his life. Patient and reliable, he carried a quiet light that still shines in my heart today.

He worked as a teacher and high school counselor. Students and colleagues respected him. He believed in his students, before they believed in themselves. Former students would stop us years later to tell him thank you—for guidance toward a career, for a steady word during a chaotic season, for encouragement when they were drifting.

One former student once told me quietly, "Your dad saved my life when I was a teenager on the verge of suicide."

My dad and I also worked part-time with the San Diego Chargers football team ticket office and summers with the Del Mar Fair. His team co-workers affectionately dubbed him, "The General," because he carried himself with wise authority and calm integrity.

Despite his long days at school and weekends at the Chargers office, he never made us feel like we were competing for his time. When he was home, he was our mentor, chauffeur, top fan (always in the audience as my musical family performed).

As a child, he was my strong hero and mentor, as an adult, my trusted friend and wise advisor. When I doubted myself—awkward and unsure—he helped me reason out the situation. He helped me find the light in the darkness as a shy and uncertain child.

My mother, practical and driven, would tell me as a child, "You need to know what you're going to be when you grow up."

My dad would gently respond, "Let her enjoy her childhood."

Although he did not often attend formal church services, his life reflected something deeply spiritual. Integrity. Compassion. Quiet sacrifice. He taught me that strength isn't loud—it's quiet consistency. It's showing up and listening. I believe he lived out the purpose God placed in him as a wonderful counselor and compassionate friend.

Though I played it safe by staying in San Diego after graduation, choosing the familiarity of a local Christian college, leaving home marked the beginning of exploring life on my own terms. Absent my parents, pets, and high school buddies, I pursued a degree in business administration. I was still not certain of my life passions but figured it was a good general degree. Another safe bet.

Living away from home was the first step to exploring my dreams and choosing spiritual faither as an adult, not just because I grew up attending church. I felt my relationship with God deepened through personal reflection, quiet conviction, and the freedom to ask my own questions.

Later in life I earned my online master's degree in public administration, while working with the City Attorney. I wanted to complete my degree in Gerontology, but the college kept cancelling classes, due to lack of sufficient student enrollment.

I wonder if completing my degree in Gerontology might have led me into my eventual ombudsman work earlier? But this advanced degree prepared me to one day be promoted to Senior Paralegal where I learned to supervise and advocate for others, growing into more responsibility.

I would later recognize those same qualities in another father across the ocean at a Ukrainian orphanage. But first, I saw them in my father. The man who could calm any storm for me.

But even lighthouses do not stand forever.

When I was in my early thirties, my father passed on from heart complications, way too soon. He was seventy years old. The man who had stood as a firm anchor in my world was gone.

His final day in the emergency room, machines hummed, far too loud, keeping his body alive. The doctors advised us they would take him off the ventilator. No hope of recovery. He could not breathe on his own. I stood by his bedside, holding his hand as I watched his chest rise and fall. I tried to memorize the rhythm of his heartbeat, as if memory alone could hold him here, in this life with me. The room felt cold, quiet except for cardiac monitors and hushed voices of staff shutting down life-support machines. The scent of disinfectant and alcohol burned my nose, yet I felt numb.

I begged God, "Please don't take my dad!"

My mom, brothers and I took turns at holding his hand, speaking gently to him. Yet his body chilled, breathing became irregular. He never regained consciousness nor spoke to us again. Once I believe his eyes opened to see my mom standing there and squeezed her hand. Or was that my imagination? But my wise advisor was physically unable to speak any final words. He passed quietly, surrounded by his family.

Without him, I felt like a lighthouse after the keeper had gone—still standing, but unsure who would tend the flame. His steady reassurance I had leaned on all my life was no longer just a phone call away.

I was grateful for my relationship with his older brother, my Uncle Si, a retired San Diego police officer. So wise and strong, like my father, yet no man could ever take my father's place.

At my father's memorial service, the room was filled beyond capacity. Students, colleagues, friends, family—standing shoulder to shoulder; heads lowered and voices hushed. Former students spoke of how this counselor inspired and encouraged them.

In the weeks that followed, the quiet was the hardest part. No more steady advice. No more calm reasoning. I wanted to reach for the phone to call him, before remembering he was gone. I would replay conversations in my mind, searching for one more piece of advice.

But I began to understand that what he had lived so naturally—his desire to help others through dark times— did not die with him. His never-ending empathy and patience would carry on. His instinct to protect the vulnerable would withstand time. His belief that each young person carries potential worth encouraging wouldn't fade without his light shining on them.

His spirit sparked something in me to also want to help others. This was the rich legacy he left in my life.

I did not know then how that lesson would prepare me to become a mentor in the Big Sister program; advocate for seniors; and canine buddy at dog shelters. I did not know how it would shape the way I would one day look into the uncertain eyes of a stray dog named Shayla. But I believe my father and God laid that foundation.

Herbert and Shirlee Bolger, Chelly's parents

Chapter Three
My Mother's Storm and Strength

If my father was the lighthouse—steady, constant, guiding—my mother, Shirlee Bolger, was the wind and storm—strong, expressive, and alive with force.

As a substitute teacher, she commanded classrooms with sharp wit and firm discipline. As an opera chorister and church soloist, she filled halls with soaring arias. At home, she moved between those worlds effortlessly—correcting homework one moment, rehearsing a choral number the next.

Growing up as her daughter was both a privilege and a trial.

In junior high, when belonging felt like survival, nothing was more mortifying than seeing my mother walk into my classroom as the no-nonsense substitute teacher. While other students groaned, I felt heat rush to my face. I wanted to vanish beneath my desk. I avoided eye contact with anyone the entire class period. Every correction she gave another student felt like it echoed back to me. I was so embarrassed.

By recess, a smirking classmate might corner me, "Do you know what your mom did to me today?"

I was often afraid to ask.

But memory softens sharp edges.

When I came home heartbroken over a teenage disappointment, my mom sometimes sat at the kitchen table for long talks. When I walked through the front door, the air often carried the buttery sweetness of fresh-baked cookies or the bright citrus scent of lemon meringue pie—the smells of home I still remember.

At night, our house hummed with music. In one room, my brothers practiced oboe and bassoon. In another, my mother sang opera or church solos, accompanying herself on the piano. Meanwhile, my father watched football or graded papers, steady and grounded beneath it all.

Occasional weekend afternoons, while my friends played in the warm sunshine, I sat in the opera hall with my dad as spectators in mom's Italian opera performances, what seemed like torture then is a treasure today.

As I grew older, independence sharpened our differences. I wanted room to explore; she wanted reassurance that I was choosing wisely. We clashed. Words spoken in frustration lingered longer than either of us intended.

And then life humbled us both.

In her later years, the woman who once commanded classrooms began to slow. Her sentences wandered as her steps became tentative. The independent spirit that had filled opera halls and church sanctuaries now needed assistance navigating hallways.

When she moved from our childhood home into independent then assisted living at a senior facility, something subtle but profound shifted. Our roles reversed, our words softened.

I reached for her hand instead of pulling away. Once daughter, now caretaker. I reminded her of appointments and listened when stories repeated. The first time I helped her fill out paperwork instead of the other way around, I felt a quiet ache in my chest. She had once tied my shoes. Now I steadied her arm in the hallways.

Love does not disappear when strength fades—it simply alters shape.

In those quiet moments beside her—far from the bustling kitchen and echoing opera halls—I saw her not as the strict substitute teacher or the driven mother pressing for answers, but as a woman who had given everything, she knew how to give: discipline, artistry, expectation, and love.

We even sang together in church choirs in those later years, sometimes joining in duets. Our voices, once divided by tension, blending in harmony.

And yet, during those same years, another quiet ache lived in my heart.

I was never blessed with children of my own. I was a stepmom for a couple of years with my first husband. I loved being an aunt to my nieces and nephew: Amanda, Kristina, Brandon, and Lexi. I joined the "Big Sister League" to mentor a young girl and was matched with my "little sister" Crystal (Kristie). Still friends today, decades later. So proud of them. But I always regretted never being a mom.

That absence does not always announce itself loudly. It settles quietly into certain holidays. Into empty bedrooms that were never filled. Into the realization that there will be no small hand reaching for yours, no one calling you "Mom."

As I cared for my aging mother, I sometimes felt the weight of that unfulfilled maternal role more deeply. I had become a caretaker—but not in the way I once imagined. Yet in that loss, God was preparing my heart to love differently—to mother through mentorship, to nurture through rescue.

When my mother passed, the silence was startling. With both of my parents gone, I now felt like an orphan. The word sounds strange when spoken by an adult—but it is real. There is something untethering about losing the two people who brought you into the world. The only ones who always knew your childhood stories by heart but are no longer present to remember the details with you.

From my mother, I inherited more than I realized in youth. Her courage to stand before an audience on stage. Her willingness to use her voice publicly. Even the discipline I once resisted became the strength I later relied upon. I learned that the relationship that challenged me most taught me strength. And I was thankful she had been my teacher.

Today, when I share Shayla's story, when I step beyond shyness and into the light, I feel both of my parents beside me. My father's steady calm. My mother's expressive voice. The lighthouse and storm, in balance.

Chapter Four
Chasing My Brothers' Light

Buzzy and Chelly

After college, I met the man who taught me what a best friend truly is. His name was Donald Wassenberg II; his friends called him "Buzzy." While my biological brothers, Bruce and Barry, shared a childhood with me, Buzzy and I bonded as he helped me find my own spirit and voice in my early 20's—it was a time of transition from college student to independent adult.

Barry and Bruce were already carving out their own paths at college in Los Angeles during my formative years. In addition to the geographic distance, our age gap of five and seven years created a natural distance. Bruce remained in Los Angeles as an attorney, which meant our time together was rare. I was proud of him, and he inspired me to pursue my career as a paralegal. Yet memories fade a bit over time and distance.

Later in life, Barry became a steady, helpful advisor and trusted friend for me—carrying forth that logical, calming, guiding light I always associated with our father. I value my family bond with him and his wife Erin, especially with the rest of our family gone or distant.

Yet, it was Buzzy who stepped into the daily spaces of my life. Just two years apart in age, he became the chosen brother in my heart. Despite his struggle for every breath against cystic fibrosis, and his busy college pursuits, he taught me to thrive on my own. I learned to stand tall while holding the hand of a brother who believed in me. He was the friend who stood beside me through every tear and heartache. A silent witness to my struggles, he taught me how to laugh at life.

We met at church, in the young adults group. You would have noticed him immediately – a tall and lean man, blond hair catching the light like sunshine on wheat. Behind thick glasses, his eyes sparkled with mischief and meaning. He was a wise old soul with an infectious laugh that lit up any room.

This young man carried himself with the quiet strength of someone who had known hardship early. Growing up on a cattle ranch in Wyoming, grit wasn't optional—it was inherited and necessary. As a child, he watched a brother die from the same cystic fibrosis disease he carried in his own lungs. Yet he refused to be defined as a "sick child."

Most people would have let that reality shrink their world. Buzzy expanded his.

He moved to San Diego alone to pursue a master's degree in genetic research. His goal was audacious and heartbreakingly personal—to help find a cure for the very illness that was slowly claiming his breath.

Buzzy laughed loudly. Loved deeply. Asked big questions. Made ridiculous jokes then explained genetic research like a master. Our late-night talks wandered from ranch life to molecular research, from suffering to sovereignty, from science to God. I still picture him, at our church, leading the children's sermon by teaching the kids how fireflies light up. The same man who enthusiastically taught me how to do the "walk like an Egyptian" dance one starry night while watching the planes land and depart at the airport.

He became my best friend. And if you've ever had a friend like that—the kind who sees you clearly and challenges you gently—you know how rare that bond is. Even more so for a man and woman with no romantic bonds.

I had grown up relatively sheltered. My world felt safe, structured, and predictable. I had never left San Diego, and just recently moved out on my own to an apartment just down the street from my parents' home. My life moved forward in familiar safe rhythms.

Buzzy's life was anything but predictable.

Every hospital stay was a reminder. Every infection, a threat. I remember sitting beside his hospital bed once, listening to the mechanical rhythm of oxygen assistance. Tubes and wires surrounded him, yet his humor remained intact. Courageously, this young scientist would give himself his own injections, claiming "staff doesn't know how to do it right." Even in weakness, he was fiercely independent.

He lived like time was chasing him, and he refused to surrender. He pushed his boundaries to live his passion.

Watching him fight for breath while striving for a cure changed me. He taught me to look beyond the physical body and into the soul. To measure life not in years, but in intention. To love a friend deeply, without reservation, even knowing loss and heartache will come.

His motto was simple and cosmic all at once: "I loved my ever-expanding universe, and those who roamed it with me."

I felt blessed to roam that world with him.

He was waiting for a lung transplant and working on his thesis when he died, as a young man in his mid-twenties. His professor finished this thesis and awarded his master's degree posthumously, a tribute to a mind that had burned brightly against narrowing time. Subsequently his research was published in a scientific journal, and a seminar series was started in Buzz's name at his alma mater.

I learned that life was not guaranteed to unfold neatly. Dreams were not promised. Death was not reserved just for seniors.

He reminded me that life, however fragile, is meant to be fully lived, with intention and enthusiasm. The transformation toward a fully lived life begins quietly. The rearview mirror holds what was safe and known. On the journey ahead lies a landscape shaped not by childhood expectations, but by intention.

I could not imagine then where that journey would eventually lead—across oceans, to a country named Ukraine and a very special dog named Shayla who would change my life.

If you are willing, come with me; find your passion and live fully.

Chapter Five
Healing a Shattered Trust

Before Shayla entered my life, there were others–companions like Buzzy who nudged open the door to my growth. Some brought joy, some pain. Each one helped me grow, realize my passion, and find myself.

While working as a bookkeeper in a locksmith shop, I met Mike, who was one of the locksmiths. Little did I know that he would change my life and test my faith. A tall, lean, dark haired, handsome man with a curly full moustache and soft brown eyes that hid the troubled spirit inside.

He was part rebel, part creative artist, a splash of color on my carefully drawn canvas. Our friendship grew, ebbed, and flowed like a sea, through seasons of doubt and devotion. Through it all, he remained one of my best friends, the one who encouraged me to think for myself and explore new avenues.

After seven years of dating, through professions of love followed by self-reliant separations, we married. Suddenly, I was "mom" to his two teenage boys living with us almost full time.

When we married, I believed that marriage was not only a commitment to a man who had been my best friend for years—but a covenant before God. I gave up on the fairytale perfect marriage long ago, yet I still believed the Lord had brought us together and would bless what we were building.

In the beginning, there was laughter. Shared plans. Conversations about the future. Vacations to Virginia and Nevada. We shared music (piano, guitar, Mike on mandolin) with family and friends. Perhaps I should have suspected something was odd though when the first night of our honey-moon in Las Vegas I woke up to find him gone and his wedding ring laying on the nightstand. The next morning, I woke up to find him there.

He said, "I just went down to gamble a bit, and I'm not used to wearing a ring yet, so it hurt my finger."

Not a man to easily settle down.

At one point we considered adopting a little girl to complete our family, in addition to his two sons, and our two tabby cats. My cat, Misty, was a lovely tabby with white stockings. We even took a few county adoption classes in preparation. But first, I begged him to adopt a dog with me, hoping this would be a first step towards adopting a child.

We started out easy—adopting a humane society black labrador puppy, Blaze (named for the white blaze on his chest), who tugged at my heart. A couple of years later, on a trip, we found a stray shepherd/aussie cattle dog puppy, Riley, lost and alone and in need of security and home. I loved him from the first moment he laid down beside me, and we became inseparable. Number one top dog!

While my marriage felt unpredictable, the dogs were my solid grounding. They did not stray or break promises. They valued consis-tency—food, structure, safety, love—and they chose to be with me.

At the time, I thought I was saving dogs. In hindsight, I realized they were also saving me.

But Mike's alcoholism became a silent third presence in our marriage. At first, it whispered, seemingly harmless. I excused it. I prayed over it. I tried to protect the image of our marriage, even as my own stability quietly eroded.

His first broken promise confused me. The first time he said he would be home by dinner and didn't come until midnight, I paced the kitchen floor pretending not to worry. I told the boys he was working late, until I got a call from the locksmith dispatch company looking for him. When he finally walked in, there was no doubt by the smell on his breath. He promised it wouldn't happen again. I wanted to believe him.

The repeated broken promises wounded me. Eventually, they betrayed something sacred. Realizing that the next drink meant more than our marriage, more than his children, and certainly more than his job or contributing a steady income.

I prayed, persevered, and hoped that my best friend and partner would return. Until God gave me clarity: love cannot compete with addiction and redemption cannot be forced. Mike refused, so I finally surrendered.

Signing those papers and filing them with the court on my fortieth birthday felt like failure, the death of a dream. I sat in my car for a long time before I entered the courthouse, debating whether I needed to file. This was not the life I imagined as a young bride at the altar.

When the clerk stamped the paperwork, the sound felt deafening. Not dramatic. Just final. No words spoken.

I returned to my car, silent and alone, and cried for what seemed like an hour. I cursed God, I screamed at Him for taking all the men who mattered most to me—Buzzy, my dad, and now Mike. I drove home alone. Blaze met me at the door. Riley leaned quietly against my leg, reminding me I was not really alone.

I felt grief—for Mike, for the friend I had loved and the man I believed he could be. Grief for what alcoholism stole from my heart and life, and his. Losing my step children and the dream of a little girl we had hoped to adopt one day. I made it clear I was keeping the house and our pups.

The betrayal I felt in Mike and myself for choosing divorce fractured something in me, not only my trust in a spouse and friend, but at times even my understanding of God.

And yet, even in that grief, I sensed something unexpected.

I realized God never left. He had been there with me through every tear, every unanswered prayer, even when I felt abandoned. And He was present in the courage it took me to ask Mike to leave our home.

But this story is not just about a failed marriage. It is about what God builds not by restoring what was, but by reshaping who we are becoming. How closed doors can redirect destiny, one step at a time.

Maybe you have stood where I stood? Perhaps you have loved someone battling something stronger than your love. Watching a dream dissolve and wondering what God was doing in the silence.

If so, you are not alone. Continue with me and see how the story that seemed like betrayal is really the beginning of something far greater in God's plan.

Chapter Six
Love, Loss, and Loyal Hearts

Blaze and Riley

After my divorce, I realized that Blaze and Riley were more than pets. They became my protectors and dear friends through some lonely days.

When I got sick with pneumonia, living alone with just a couple female roommates, Blaze and Riley became my constant companions. My roommates took them out for potty and feeding, but otherwise they rested quietly on the bed beside me. I felt their love gave me strength to recover, not just to play with them again, but to heal inside and out.

Blaze was strength—bold, alert, always aware, my funny little clown. Riley was steadiness—present, intuitive, deeply attuned. Together, they formed a kind of living reassurance that I was not alone.

Some dogs share your house. Some share your routines. And occasionally—if you are fortunate—one is truly your "canine soulmate."

Riley was that dog for me. He seemed to understand me in a way nobody else could. He did not try to solve anything. He simply stayed by my side, through joy, sadness, and illness.

Blaze and Riley were the bridge between the life I was leaving and the life I hadn't yet imagined. And in that in-between place—where everything felt both fragile and possible—I met George at church. A tall, lean, handsome, blonde man who had endured his own physical hardship and childhood trauma. This man was a stark contrast from my prior relations. He took pride in his landscaping, and later wood crafting creations. Most of all, he proved reliable, trustworthy, and committed to hearth and home.

When I married George, Blaze and Riley accepted him in a way that felt like their blessing. They had guarded me through one chapter of my life, and now they were walking with us into another. They became his friends too. He laughed at Blaze's boldness and humor. He welcomed Riley's constant presence. We were a family.

Years later, Riley was diagnosed with cancer and shortly after, Blaze was diagnosed with a tumor. I was heartbroken. It was as though the very protectors who had carried me through so much were now facing something I could not fight for them.

When their bodies began to fail in ways dignity could no longer hide, I faced that heartbreaking moment many pet parents fear. Loving them meant facing the moment when holding on would become selfish and letting go would become the final act of love.

Our family and friends who had loved "the boys" gathered at our home on their last night. Our pastor came to bless them. Mike even came by one last time to say goodbye to them.

My boys had walked through those years together. It felt fitting, though unbearably painful, that they would leave together too. We spoiled them with all their favorite treats on their last day.

That fateful summer day, George and I gathered with them on our back patio as our veterinarian and her tech arrived. As we prepared to say goodbye, George and I placed our hands steady on them. The air was still and warm that summer afternoon. Too still. We spread a soft blanket in the exact place they loved to rest on the back patio. Blaze rested his head in George's lap. Riley pressed against me, as he always had.

The veterinarian spoke gently, explaining each step. I barely heard her. I memorized the feel of their fur beneath my fingers. I whispered gratitude for every year, every walk, every quiet night they stood guard over me.

One by one, with each final injection, their breathing slowed. As their spirits flew away, into God's waiting arms, the One who created them took them home.

The vet and tech carried their bodies, wrapped in soft blankets, out to their car. The world paused as two chapters of my life closed. I sat on our back patio, in tears, as two beautiful orange butterflies drifted past my eyes. I felt their message: "It's okay, they are safe with God now."

Losing Blaze was painful, but losing Riley at the same time was shattering. Losing him felt like losing the keeper of my memories; like an era of my life had ended.

The house afterward seemed overwhelmingly silent. No paws crossed the kitchen floor. No familiar weight pressed against my legs. Their beds lay untouched; their bowls stacked away.

I told myself I could not do it again. I could not open my heart to something that would one day leave.

But love has a way of asking us to risk. Again.

We did not last more than a couple of months before we knew we needed another canine companion. Our search began. Our shepherd/malamute Juneau came into our lives softly. Shy. Unsure. Shelter staff advised he had been in a domestic violence home, affected by trauma. Where Blaze had been bold and Riley steady, Juneau was cautious. He startled easily. Trust did not come quickly. Just like me as a shy child.

Loving him required extra patience. I sat on the floor and waited. I softened my voice. I celebrated small victories—a hesitant step forward, a tail wag, a moment of eye contact.

Honey, Juneau, Chelly and George

By then, George and I were building our life together in practical ways too. I was the primary breadwinner, in a decades-long, secure San Diego City Attorney's Office paralegal career while George tried to build his landscape company. His physical limitations and inconsistent work meant I carried more of the financial burden, blessed to have steady work.

Some days that responsibility felt heavy. Some days I felt the strain of being the one who had to hold everything steady. But God always gives enough strength for the day. So, while I worked, I also focused on rescue, for me and for Juneau.

We brought Honey home from the local humane society, not only because we wanted another dog, but because our shy Juneau did.

Honey was my first strong female. No longer a puppy but a six-year-old yellow labrador. Confident. Grounded. She entered our home as though she had always belonged. Where Juneau hesitated, Honey stood firm. Where Juneau flinched, Honey leaned in.

Watching Honey steady Juneau was like watching strength shelter fragility. They bonded as inseparable friends. On one of our first walks together, Juneau startled at a passing bicycle. Honey did not flinch. She simply stood still, then looked back at him as if to say, "It's okay." Slowly, he stepped forward. I realized she was teaching him bravery in a language only dogs speak. Similar to how my dad's confident and quiet strength taught me bravery.

But time, as always, passed by too quickly. Honey's vibrant energy slowly faded, and despite veterinarian care, a healing natural food and supplements regimen, and lots of love, her body began to fail. She suffered from a stroke at age thirteen and soon life took our sweet Honey.

Honey's passing left a different kind of silence. After she was gone, the house felt off balance. Juneau felt it most. The night we came home after putting Honey down, Juneau laid quietly on her blanket, beside her empty crate.

I learned that when I gripped life too tightly—clinging to my pre-conceived notion of safety—I often missed what was next in God's plan. I did not know yet that my heart and our home were being prepared for a dog whose story began in a country across the ocean.

Chapter Seven

Igniting My Passion Through Rescue

Bolton and Chelly

Without Honey's quiet assurance, Juneau drifted again into uncertainty. He stood with his tail tucked and ears flat. He followed us more closely. He needed a companion who understood what it meant to be displaced and grieving.

Volunteering in animal shelters, notably a greyhound rescue, a senior dog rescue, and a county humane society, changed me. The faces of the unchosen, the overlooked, the broken, and the aging imprinted themselves on my heart.

Boltan, a white shepherd living at a rescue, previously discarded by his owner as he aged, touched my heart. I thought of his snowy white coat against cold kennel walls. I remembered the way he leaned into my hand, steady, and hopeful. I wanted to bring him home, but he did not seem the best match with Juneau. I felt so sad I could not provide a "forever home" for him. But for now, love meant taking him out on special trips; showing up until someone else could provide him the best home to meet his needs.

My shelter shepherd widened my understanding of what it meant to care. Rescue had changed the way I saw the world. I no longer wondered, *Which dog fits neatly into our lives?* Instead, I found myself praying, *Lord, show me how to help those who need me most.*

I heard stories of actual rescued animals that broke my heart; others that infuriated me. I visited the forgotten ones—greyhounds curled up against cold steel cage bars, unwanted after losing their final track races; traumatized and scarred pups rescued from brutal dog-fighting rings.

I knelt to comfort misunderstood and abandoned gentle pit bulls like Snowflake and Pita, who were despised by some solely because of their breed. Eventually some would just go crazy from confinement, beyond hope of rescue, and be put down to make room for new souls.

My initial fear, uncertainty, pain, the feeling that I was too busy, too educated to "settle for social work and menial pay" (as my mom once termed my desire to earn my college degree in social advocacy) transformed quickly once I started volunteering with dog rescue groups. Like I had been in a dark room and a light switched on. I found resolve and purpose, simply by getting involved.

What once felt like coincidence began to feel like His calling—as though God had been arranging these encounters long before I understood why.

Years earlier, I had volunteered as a Big Sister and spent time visiting seniors in long term care facilities. Even then, I felt drawn to those who seemed overlooked. But eventually that quiet pull grew into something more defined. Advocacy was no longer something I did on the side; it became my new career path.

I directed my paralegal research and supervisor skills to work as a state ombudsman specialist. Walking into long-term care facilities not as a visitor, but as a representative to empower residents who could no longer advocate for themselves. I spoke with people who felt forgotten; some who had forgotten who they once were. My role was to remind them—and the facility managers—of their resident rights.

One resident I met, another San Diego career transplant who loved dogs, with a sharp wit but failing body, once whispered, "You're the first person who has really listened in a long time." Her words stayed with me. She reached for my hand as she said it. Her room was small, decorated with faded photos of a younger woman and a book she wrote about her experiences with shepherd dogs. Her body had weakened, but her mind was sharp.

The same longing I had seen in shelter dogs—the need to be seen, valued, and chosen—was present with people too. And slowly I began

to recognize the pattern. The overlooked kept appearing in my path —
and I began to feel that God was asking me to see them and care.

*Finding our way on our self-discovery journey seems to come one step at
a time.* There was no trumpet fanfare announcing I was on the "right
path." It unfolded quietly. A shelter dog decided to finally trust people
again, to trust me, when other rescuers said "wow, he has not trusted
anyone else." This was just the beginning, sparking an ever-present
passion for rescue, from quiet embers to dancing flames.

Chapter Eight
Let Shayla's Adventure Begin

Now that I have laid the foundation for this adventure in self-discovery, destination chosen, bags packed, it's time for that journey to begin. Introducing Shayla, my muse, my companion, and the answer to a whispered prayer. Who is your inspiration?

A muse is someone or something that sparks creativity, a source of inspiration. But a muse doesn't just inspire—they awaken something sacred. As God began opening doors of new experiences in my life, to lead me to a place of compassion and serving others, despite my uncertainty, the time was right for Shayla, and an orphanage across the world, to touch my heart.

I continued volunteering with local rescues, secretly considering any possible dogs for a match with us. I patiently scrolled through pet adoption ads in search of a dog to complete our family. I knew Juneau needed a buddy. George, ever practical, needed a bit more time to agree. But eventually he realized too how much we ALL needed to take that next step again.

Over the next couple of months, with Juneau in tow, we met several rescue dogs. None felt quite right. We kept searching.

Then one evening, while scrolling through adoption listings, a photo stopped me.

Her name was Layla—we would later rename her Shayla. A female shepherd mix with soulful eyes and something ancient in her gaze. Staff believed she was born in December 2017. Her watchful intelligence and quiet strength seemed to reach through the screen. She looked almost like Juneau's cousin. The description said she liked other dogs and was in good health, up to date on vaccinations. But it was her gaze that held our attention.

I was excited and nervous at the same time. I submitted the application and prayed softly. Lord, if this is the one, make it clear.

One magical night in November 2020, I got that call I will never forget from Sarah, one of the rescue volunteers at Amazing Strays Rescue in San Diego. She told me the rescue received several applications for Layla, but mine stood out because I had a lot of experience as a dog volunteer and a German Shepherd owner.

But there was a twist—Layla wasn't in San Diego. She was in Ukraine, and Sarah had never met the dog. Wait, WHAT???

Ukraine? I had never traveled farther than Mexico. I had never heard of a Czechoslovakian wolfdog, This felt very different from adopting from a local shelter. It was not the kind of adoption story I had imagined.

I wondered, "What if this is a scam, what if it doesn't work out? What if she is not healthy or is too wild to accept us?"

And yet—the door felt open.

I was perplexed and asked, "How are you advertising a dog for rescue that you don't even have?"

Sarah explained, "My father, Bruce Elliott, a San Diego businessman, helped bring at least fifteen other rescue dogs from a Ukrainian orphanage here, partnering with Father's House to bring them to safety."

I questioned how Bruce got involved with a Ukrainian orphanage.

She told me, "He was a long-term board member, co-founder, and supporter of Father's House. We were told Layla helped raise puppies and comforted orphan children, while waiting for her forever home."

Sounded like a good and happy dog. I asked about her physical health, living in a foreign land.

Again, Sarah shared the right answers to our relief. "She was certified in good health by a veterinarian in Ukraine and has her own passport."

Wow, I didn't even have a passport then.

Sarah told me that another family previously adopted a similar looking dog from the orphanage and ran a DNA test which indicated that the dog was a Shepherd/Czechoslovakian Wolfdog. She said, "Shayla could be the same breed. She might be a Czechoslovakian Wolfdog."

I laughed, God, you do have a sense of humor. Exotic Wolfdog? But I remembered our malamute Juneau, and how the rare ones always found me. The only knowledge I had then was that dogs descended from wolves at some point in their evolution. I knew about German Shepherds, but now I set out to learn about Czechoslovakian Wolfdogs and what we had just agreed to adopt!

Thanksgiving approached, and so did Shayla's arrival. Sarah called me two days prior to ask one final question: "Are you ready, and still interested?"

With cautious optimism, I told Sarah, "Yes, we want her...if Juneau approves."

Our world was about to change forever; in ways we never imagined. A dog from across the globe. A doorway into a foreign culture and world we had never imagined. But one we would come to genuinely love. For a couple without children, our hearts were about to embrace an entire orphanage family. We even became sponsors later for a young child at Father's House.

We decided to let the adventure begin—led by faith, shaped by love, and inspired by one special Ukrainian dog.

Chapter Nine
The Spirit of a Shepherd/Wolfdog

Shayla at Goldwater Lake

Sometimes, my college and paralegal research background still surface before I make a final decision. I trust God, but old habits die hard. Every wise traveler studies the path before starting forth. We check maps, learn the climate and landmarks, and pack accordingly. Love may inspire the journey, but preparation protects

I prepared for Shayla's adoption the same way.

I immersed myself in everything I could find about the Czechoslovakian Wolfdog—the Vlcak—and German Shepherd mixes. I wasn't just adopting a dog. I was preparing to enter her world.

The Vlcak is strikingly wolf-like in face and posture, bred in the 1950s from German Shepherds and Carpathian wolves for border patrol work in Czechoslovakia. Designed for endurance, intelligence, and loyalty, they possess marathon stamina, heightened senses, and a deep bond with their families. Independent. Alert. Not a breed for the unprepared.

That both excited and sobered me.

These dogs require consistency, early socialization, and patient leadership. Not typically recommended for first-time owners or families with small children. I smiled at that. Shayla had grown up around children at Father's House. For me, years with German Shepherds, guidance from our trainer Rob, and my time with the San Diego Humane Society had quietly equipped us.

Even nutrition became part of the packing list. Experts recommended a natural, raw diet. I remembered Riley's remarkable improvement years earlier after switching to whole foods and supplements. The Vlcak's average lifespan of around fifteen years felt like grace.

The more we learned, the more we knew we wanted her. Shayla would not simply be another rescue. She carried instinct and independence in her bloodline—wolf and shepherd woven together. Strength and sensitivity. Wildness and devotion.

Like any careful traveler, we studied the path laid out before us. Research prepared us. But love—especially the kind God weaves into our lives—eventually asks for trust beyond what facts can guarantee. In many aspects of my life, I had played it safe. At some point, we simply had to take that first step—trusting that God, who had led us this far, would continue to guide us.

And in that quiet, steady faith, we knew we were ready to welcome Shayla.

Chapter Ten
A Fond Farewell to Ukraine

At the airport leaving Ukraine

Back in Ukraine, at Father's House, young Shayla had grown. She was a beloved dog, a favorite of many orphanage children and staff. Roman, the orphanage founder and manager, along with his wife Natasha, and adult daughters Alina and Anastasia, had raised Shayla at Father's House from a puppy.

Still, Shayla watched as other dogs left with strangers, tails wagging, eyes bright. They never returned. She must have wondered, *Will someone ever come for me?*

Roman would later share with us the solemn promise he made to Shayla. 'One day, a forever family will come for you, sweet girl,' he assured her. 'Just be patient and wait on God's timing.'

Seasons passed. Snow melted into spring. Puppies arrived and left. Shayla remained.

Then one day, in November 2022, everything changed.

Alina knelt beside Shayla, her voice trembling with both joy and sorrow. "You're going on a journey," she whispered. "A long one—to America."

The word meant nothing to Shayla, but Alina's tears did.

Mykola, the little orphan boy who originally rescued Shayla, crouched beside her, pressing his forehead to hers. "Your scars made you strong," he said softly. "I love you enough to let you go." His voice broke. "Be brave."

Shayla leaned into him, licking the tears from his cheek.

In the following weeks, the dogs were examined by a veterinarian and issued passports. Early one cold November morning, the children gathered for one last goodbye. There were tight hugs, whispered prayers, and tears falling onto soft fur.

Then came the crates.

Roman guided Shayla inside. "Trust me," he said quietly. She complied.

The crates were loaded into a van and driven to the airport. Before her crate disappeared down the conveyor belt, Roman leaned close. One more promise. "You will be okay girl. Sleep for a while. You will wake up in a safer place."

Then darkness. Engines. The unfamiliar roar of flight. The plane began to taxi and accelerate down the runway, shaking her crate. She likely heard soft whimpers from her canine friends, nearby in their crates.

No sedatives were given, for fear of what "could" happen physically without an attendant. For thirteen long hours from Ukraine to Los Angeles, the dogs endured the noise and confinement, although the cargo hold was pressurized and climate controlled. Shayla could not stretch her long legs. She could only wait. Somewhere above the clouds, in the belly of a metal bird, Shayla surrendered to the unknown.

Though she was leaving the only home she had known, I believe she was still held in God's care.

This was not just Shayla's journey. It was a story of trusting when the road ahead cannot be seen—and of believing that the One who calls us to leave also prepares the place we are going.

Chapter Eleven
Crossing the Bridge to America

Crossing from Ukraine to America

When Shayla woke, the world was different.

Gone were the familiar scents and voices of Father's House. Instead, strangers in uniforms moved around her crate, speaking a language she did not know. Her dog companions were nearby, but Alina, Mykola, and the children were not.

Eventually she heard something familiar—Roman's voice. Bruce's laugh. Tails thumped. Ears perked. The dogs answered in a chorus of hopeful barking.

Bruce and Roman took the dogs out of their crates and guided them outside to the parking lot, stepping into the moonless night of Los Angeles, illuminated by various lights. The cool air here smelled different—scents of people, metal, asphalt, car exhaust, and salty ocean spray. There were so many people. After a long wait and a quick stretch, they were loaded into vans for the drive south to San Diego. For Shayla, it would be her first night sleeping inside a real home.

The next morning, Bruce opened the car door—and Shayla confidently leapt into the front passenger seat. Roman chuckled and slid into the back. She was ready for adventure.

Meanwhile, at our ranch home in Lakeside, George and I were preparing. A crate lined with soft blankets. Plush toys. Treats. A sign that read, "Welcome Home Shayla"—officially changing her name from Layla. Juneau, freshly bathed and sporting a new blue collar, same style as Shayla's. We all waited with quiet curiosity.

When Bruce's car pulled up, I spied from the window and saw her—sitting tall and lean in the front passenger seat, beautiful and exotic. Those large ears. That alert, wolf-like grace.

I ran to get George, proclaiming "She's so cute. This has to work out."

Once Bruce and Roman exited the car, with Shayla on a soft leash, we greeted each other nervously. Roman spoke very limited English, but Bruce was able to interpret for us all. I think after Shayla's long journey, we were all hoping this match would work.

I knelt and offered my open hand to Shayla, under her chin, and said hello. Her golden eyes met mine—wild and gentle at once. She allowed us to pet her, but her attention quickly turned to mapping the yard, moving with curious elegance.

Bruce said, "She has a hopeful, sweet disposition, and positive outlook at all times, even as a stray. She is very smart." What a perfect description.

Shayla stepped forward with cautious grace, her slender frame alert but not tense, her nose twitching as she took in the scents of her new surroundings.

Juneau stood nearby, tail wagging in slow, deliberate arcs. He didn't rush her. He simply waited, his posture open, his eyes soft. When Shayla noticed him, she paused. Their gaze met—two souls, both rescued, both softened by human tenderness. She took a few steps toward him, then stopped. He mirrored her. It was a silent dance of trust, the beginning of a beautiful friendship.

In the afternoon warmth, Juneau found a patch of cool ground under our old tree and began digging a hole. Shayla watched his endeavor with growing interest. Then, with a playful sparkle in her eye, she trotted over and pounced onto the same hole to join in his fun, sending a flurry of dust skyward.

Juneau froze, ears tilted and eyes wide, and looked at her as if to say, "What are you doing – this is MY hole." But true to his gentle nature, he did not growl or protest. Instead, he wagged his tail slowly, and a look of surprise and amusement passed between them. If dogs can laugh, they surely did. Shayla had just rewritten the rules of canine friendship, one dusty pawprint at a time.

George and I exchanged a glance, the kind that says everything without words. This was the moment we'd prayed for—not just a dog arriving, but a connection forming, for us and the dogs.

Shayla circled the yard once more, then trotted back to us, her ears perked and her tail lifted in a gentle curve. She leaned into my leg, just slightly, and I felt the warmth of her fur against my jeans. She chose us, just as much as we chose her. That's the way with real friends.

Bruce nodded approvingly. "She's ready," he said. "She knows this is her next chapter."

As we walked the yard perimeter, the trainer who came with Bruce pointed out a few things to watch for (pointing out low hanging branches near the five-foot chain-link fence), cautioning us that Shayla's Czech wolfdog traits came with a spirited blend of curiosity, agility, and boundless energy. We smiled, secretly thinking she was exaggerating. We would come to know this was no exaggeration, though not exactly what the trainer warned us about.

After our pack walk, we all went inside and showed Shayla her new home. Bruce read the "Welcome Home" sign on Shayla's crate to Roman, who smiled in agreement that this was a good home for his friend. Assured the dogs were fine together, and with George and I just awestruck by Shayla, we agreed we wanted her. We spoke a bit longer with Bruce and Roman, eager to learn every bit of information about Shayla and her life.

Finally it was time, Bruce handed me Shayla's leash.

It felt symbolic—more than nylon and metal. A thread of trust passed from one heart to another.

Before leaving, Roman knelt beside her, speaking softly in Ukrainian. He cupped her face in his hands, tears slipping down his cheeks. She listened, still and attentive. A private goodbye between two souls who understood sacrifice.

Roman let go, but not without leaving a piece of himself behind. My new friend and his life story touched my heart and inspired me, just as my own father once had. Watching Roman trust God so fully stirred something in me. I wanted that kind of steady faith.

Roman and Bruce were such kind and good-hearted Christian men. I think they knew that from that day forward, they and Shayla would carry a piece of each other's heart, and that true friendship lasts forever.

Bruce translated Roman's words, "We love Shayla, and we know that God does too. I believe you will provide the best home for her." Bruce and Roman both hugged Shayla, said their good-byes, then departed.

Then the van disappeared down the long road. A quiet stillness filled the air.

Shayla stood watching, ears forward, body poised between past and future. She turned toward me, her golden eyes soft but searching, as if trying to understand the shift in her world.

I knelt beside her, touching her shoulder. "Welcome home, sweetheart. We're so happy you're here."

She leaned into my leg.

She had crossed an invisible bridge between two worlds. From a stray puppy in Ukraine, full of hope and promise, and arrived safely in America, with Roman's promise of a good new life about to start.

Later that evening, as the sun dipped behind the trees and the ranch settled into its usual hush, Shayla curled up near Juneau, not in her crate, but beside him on the living room rug. They didn't touch, but they were already accepting each other and becoming companions.

And as I sat nearby, heart full, I thought of Roman—his tearful goodbye, his whispered blessings. I hoped he could feel the peace of this moment, wherever he was. I also wondered how Alina and Mykola must feel about Shayla being so far away. I hoped Roman would tell them that she found a good home and family. And I prayed that one day we would have that deep emotional connection with her, like Roman.

I am pleased that I am still in regular online contact with Roman and his daughters Alina and Anastasia. still sharing updates and Shayla photos. I am happy to visit Bruce and Anne, usually once a year, frequently with Shayla. I dream of going to Ukraine one day to see Father's House in person.

I never imagined the adventure that began for all of us that day she came to live with us. We prayed and thanked God, "Although this was not the family or life that Shayla was born into, help us be the forever family that You want her to be with."

Chapter Twelve
The Favored Orphanage Puppy

Shayla as a puppy with kitten friend

After Shayla arrived, Bruce and Alina provided us with the details of Shayla's life in Ukraine. Prior to joining our family, Shayla's story began on the streets of Petrivske, a village in Ukraine's Kiev-Svyatoshinsky district, a rural area about an hour south of Kiev.

In the light of Ukraine's economic and humanitarian struggles, the fate of one stray puppy might have seemed insignificant. In many ways, Shayla's resilience mirrored the strength I would later come to see in the Ukrainian people as I got to know the Korniyko family and other Ukrainian supporters like the folks at San Diego's House of Ukraine.

The streets of Ukraine were surely a scary and lonely world for a puppy. They roared with traffic, echoed with the growls of larger, territorial dogs, and bustled with people too burdened to notice a small, hungry puppy.

Hunger gnawed at her belly, but she feared people. Shayla scavenged what she could—bits of food, puddles of water as the cold air bit her nose—never enough, always uncertain. She preferred to watch people from a safe distance, out of clear view. On cold nights, she searched for shelter beneath stairwells, tucked into tight spaces out of sight.

Although an attractive black and tan puppy with a cute white tail tip, she could not compete by charm alone with so many stray dogs and homeless people. To most, she was just another problem, another shadow.

One day she took a chance. She befriended a young Ukrainian boy named Mykola Yuhimenko. Like Shayla, Mykola had lost his family at a young age and was alone in the world. He approached her slowly and sat beside her quietly over a few days, waiting for her to approach him. He left small scraps of food on the floor until she accepted it from him by hand. He would play ball with her, slowly building her trust as they became good friends. Each day he returned to check on her until that one morning she lingered and approached him cautiously. Mykola extended his hand slowly and she licked his face.

Although Shayla didn't trust Mykola at first, he understood her caution. It seemed that God, with infinite wisdom, brought these two lives together, and Mykola said he "loved Shayla instantly because she was so cute."

Their bond grew quickly, rooted in shared loneliness and loving hearts seeking companionship. The bridge from fear to belonging is rarely crossed in a single leap. It is built step by step—kindness by kindness.

Mykola grew up and worked at the Christian orphanage, "Father's House" and knew Roman and his adult daughters, Alina and Anastasia, welcomed homeless dogs as companions for the children. So, he brought Shayla to his home there, knowing she would be welcomed. The Korniyko family embraced her with open arms, folding her into a life filled with children, kindness, and other rescued animals. As she grew up, the orphanage became her sanctuary.

Shayla grew up lean and long, graceful in movement, and gentle in spirit, loved by the children. Shayla loved to play with them whenever she could, chasing the balls they threw for her and running about the yard together. Her presence was more than playful though, it was healing. She gave love freely, without judgment, and in return, the children loved and healed her sad heart. Often, a small hand reached out to pet her soft fur or scratch her white tummy. Sometimes a child would curl up beside Shayla, drifting off to peaceful sleep; safety and love wrapped around them both like a cozy blanket.

Shayla quickly grew attached to Roman's family and the rhythm of life at Father's House. Alina, with her quiet devotion, became Shayla's caretaker and teacher. She fed her what she could, taught her commands like "Day Lapu"—a Ukrainian phrase meaning "give me your paw," and praised her intelligence with every new skill learned. Alina informed me that Shayla wasn't just a pet; she found purpose in the orphanage by assisting Alina in mentoring the younger puppies, guiding them with patience and poise, as if she understood the importance of her role.

She also told me that Shayla was a favorite of the children. "She would curl up beside a sad child, paw softly touching their small hand, and lean in close to soften their tears."

But Mykola remained her closest companion. Some days, they wandered the village together, playfully exploring. Other days, they just sat side by side as Mykola would open his heart to confide how he was also an orphan. At Father's House, for the first time, he learned that God loved him and accepted him, unconditionally, that his life had value. Roman also encouraged him to be good, care about others, taught him skills, and provided for his needs. Roman became like a father to him and so many other children.

Although Shayla loved her family, she still had a bit of a wild instinct that made her wary of fully trusting people. She wanted to teach and educate her new Ukrainian family how to honor her boundaries. Sometimes, she still longed to roam independently on an adventure, to follow her instincts and explore the world on her own terms. Yet she always returned.

Her home was also filled with dogs of all shapes and temperaments, and even a few curious cats who dared to play. Shayla welcomed them all—young or old, bold, or timid, able-bodied, or differently abled. She saw past appearances and met each creature with acceptance.

Sometimes another dog, Lizze, would join Shayla in bolting and running through the fields into town, carefree and wild, chasing lizards and rabbits along the way, testing the boundaries of their world.

The dogs learned which strangers in town might be kind to them and offer scraps of food with kind words.

But, no matter how far they roamed, they always returned to the safety of Father's House. Though a scolding might await them, or they might not be allowed to run free again for a while, the joy of running wild made it all worthwhile. Imaginably even then, she knew there was something more waiting—her forever home. Alina and Anastasia would laugh at their determined carefree spirits, hug them, and welcome them home. Hearing later about how Shayla and Lizze would run and return leaves me to wonder if we humans aren't the same—wandering yet always hoping for God's open arms to welcome us back home once again when we stray.

Life at Father's House was safe, although not always easy. Shayla's freedom was limited. When no one had time to spend with the dogs, they were tied up or confined into a small, fenced enclosure for their safety, sometimes for many hours. They were not allowed to go outside the enclosure, even on potty breaks. Food was scarce at times, limited to scraps and tiny bites. Those were some difficult days, yet she never lost her gentle heart.

Bruce, Roman, and his family saw the need, not just for shelter, but for true belonging. They dreamed of something more for Shayla and the other dogs: a life where they would find warmth, ample provision, and be treasured companions, with their own forever families.

Shayla's journey was far from over, but the promise of a forever home was beginning to take shape. Her dream destination was visible on the horizon now. Like a weary traveler's first glimpse of their intended vacation spot.

This is not just Shayla's journey—it's ours. A story of waiting, of trusting, of letting go. A story of being led, even when we cannot see the road ahead. And always, God is our pilot on this journey.

Chapter Thirteen

God's Divine Plan for Father's House

Roman Korniyko and Bruce Elliott

Long before we ever prayed for Shayla, God was working in ways we couldn't see. The best people who would rescue and love her as a young dog became her rescue network.

I was also interested to learn more about Shayla's Ukrainian family at Father's House (Otchiy Dim). Some details would come later as we forged a caretaker's bond with Bruce and the Korniyko family. Together Roman, his family, and Bruce orchestrated an incredible journey—one that brought Shayla, and many other dogs, safely to forever homes in America.

Roman Korniyko was once a promising young medical doctor in Ukraine, married and the father of two daughters, Anastasia and Alina. His journey took a turn, over twenty-five years ago, not through ambition, but through prayer. In the midst of a personal crisis, Roman pleaded with God to restore his failing marriage and protect his family. He prayed that his daughters would not grow up without their father.

Roman described a moment when his heart shifted and compassion for Ukraine's forgotten children became impossible to ignore. "When God answered my prayers, I offered my heart and life in service to God—and God opened my eyes to the suffering of others around me."

He never imagined leaving his medical career to work with orphans and the homeless. But when God's divine love flooded Roman's heart for Ukraine's forgotten people and abandoned children, his life forever changed.

Roman surrendered his dream of becoming the youngest medical professor in his country. He surrendered his medical ambitions, believing God was asking something different of him. He did so with solemn gratitude that God chose him to serve His children. Roman's new calling was clear: "to be a father to the fatherless." To offer hope where there had been betrayal. To rewrite the stories of children who had known only trauma.

As Roman has said, "Whatever you dedicate your life to for Jesus is eternal, and you take that with you into eternity. Discover what that purpose is for you and follow the value in that."

Roman's life became proof that fulfillment doesn't always come from worldly possessions or success, but from obedience to what God places before you. He believed that when he stepped forward in faith, God would meet him there—and time after time, provision arrived in unexpected ways.

He once told an interviewer, "If you pursue God's plan with your whole heart, God will create the miracles to fulfill the dream."

In the early 1990s, Ukraine declared independence from the Soviet Union. The country was in turmoil: economic collapse, high unemployment, political corruption, widespread alcoholism, drug addiction, abuse, and certain depression. Bandits often raided homes, sometimes killing the parents and leaving children orphaned. Two percent of Ukraine's kids were orphaned, left alone to run the streets in gangs, begging for food scraps.

Roman began walking the streets of his local Ukrainian community to see first-hand the appalling conditions and meet these children face-to-face. They invited him into their hidden world of makeshift shelters in barren areas under buildings with scavenged mattresses and household items, underground communities with no parents or family support, cold and alone. He saw where the kids would punch holes in the underground water pipes for a trickle of water to shower. He knew he could not turn away from these young lives.

He invited a few of these orphans to his home. He offered showers, clean clothes, food, and safe shelter. Although nervous about exposing his young daughters to unknown dangers, he trusted that God would protect them all. God proved faithful, and his daughters were never ill. Soon, his modest two-bedroom apartment (equivalent to 1 bedroom plus a living room in Ukraine) was home to ten orphans joining his family. Then he rented out a second small apartment, housing an additional eighteen orphans.

Roman, through Anastasia, told of a day that police stormed into the Korniyko apartment to arrest a boy wanted by juvenile authorities. The boy offered to surrender, and by a miracle, the police officer pleaded with the judge to allow the boy to complete community service rather than face arrest.

The officer took Roman before the town's mayor and said, "These are the people who change children's lives." The mayor responded by offering a larger facility, and Father's House grew to shelter over thirty orphans.

Although resources were scarce, Roman's faith and ministry never faltered. After three days of fasting and prayer for a larger facility to serve the orphans, God provided another miracle. A friend called to say a woman's mother had passed away, leaving money to be used for a deserving charity. She offered Roman those funds to buy a larger home for the children. The amount matched exactly the cost of the home Roman hoped to buy, their current beloved "blue house" in Ukraine.

Badly in need of restoration, it served as a sanctuary where they could all live together. Painted in cheerful blues, its exterior walls adorned with playful animals.

Father's House, under Roman's direction and assisted by his devoted family, continued to grow and expand services. They provided invaluable charitable service within their community for homeless children, seniors, and even animals. They created a series of programs designed to create a path to societal integration for the children. Instead of cold institutions, a home was built, based on a positive family-oriented structure, rehabilitation, and teaching the children their value in society. Finally, the children had "parents" and teachers to exemplify to them the goodness of a family and to teach them about God's love and protection. The Ukrainian economy was starting to improve, and the people were proud, resilient, and educated.

The orphanage earned national recognition and numerous awards as a foundation for social reform in Ukraine. Numerous churches and humanitarian service groups rallied behind it. One such group is Ezra International Ukraine, a Christian non-profit dedicated to rescuing and restoring abused, neglected, and abandoned children in that country. Bruce Elliott, Chairman of the Ezra International Father's House Board and Director of Ezra International Ukraine Children's Work, and his wife Anne became staunch supporters and friends of Roman over twenty years ago, assisting in the rescue of children and animals.

Their story is one of miracles, sacrifice, faith, and discovered passion. and unwavering faith. And it's the world that shaped the gentle, soulful dog Shayla who would become part of our family.

Shayla and Mykola

Alina and Shayla

The Children and Shayla at Father's House

Shayla and Friends at Father's House

Chapter Fourteen
Shayla Joins the Pack

Shayla, Juneau, Shelly and George

Well, I wish I could say that Shayla was always the good girl Roman told her to be. But that would not be the full truth. She seemed content and happy in her new life with us, enjoying the attention of her own human "Mom" and "Dad," and playing with her big brother Juneau.

Yet behind her sweet demeanor pulsed the heart of a wanderer, one who could not fully settle into domestic life. Freedom ran in her blood. Fortunately, so did loyalty.

Every so often, the call of the canyon proved irresistible, and she longed for a new adventure. With a mischievous twinkle in her eye, Shayla would dig under the fence to run through the neighboring open canyon. She seemed to vanish into the wild expanse, chasing rabbits and lizards like a wild dog, just like in Ukraine.

Her biggest problem was that she could only get under the fence one way, not back under. George and I got to know our neighbors well. Lesson learned. Never underestimate a wolfdog with ambition!

Shayla's flair for drama didn't end at the fence line. Trips to the vet or groomer for nail trims became theatrical events. The moment a technician so much as lifted her paw, she'd unleash a banshee wail that echoed through the building. Heads turned. Conversations paused. And there I was, red-faced, murmuring apologies to the staff and fellow pet parents. "Yes," I'd sigh, "that drama queen is mine." They'd smile kindly, but I knew Shayla had made a lasting impression.

Juneau and Shayla became good friends quickly, their bond forged not just in shared walks and sun-drenched naps, but in the quiet understanding that comes when two souls recognize each other.

Our aging malamute welcomed his young charge with patient dignity. Where she was motion, he was wisdom. Where she tested limits, he modeled them. He didn't need to bark commands—his calm presence was enough. Shayla, ever observant, watched and learned.

Together, they became a study in harmony and balance. Side by side, they shared in discovering new adventures. Their friendship reminded me that wisdom isn't measured in years, and connection doesn't require matching speeds. With friends of different ages, cultures, and physical capabilities, my life (and Shayla's) expanded in wonderful ways. Side by side, they moved in a rhythm that balanced energy with wisdom. Watching them, I was reminded that connection isn't built on sameness. It thrives on complement. My life—and Shayla's—grew richer through relationships that crossed age, personality, and even species.

Shayla especially loves children. I felt her time near the orphanage left its imprint. She is gentle with adults, but when a child approaches, something in her softens further. Her tail wags a little faster. Her eyes brighten. She leans in carefully, confidently, as if greeting an old friend.

It was possible she remembered the laughter of children from her early days. Or maybe children and dogs simply share a language all their own—one rooted in presence, curiosity, and wholehearted living.

Like travelers who discover that the richest experiences come not from rushing through destinations but from sitting still long enough to truly connect, Shayla appears to understand something simple and profound: that belonging grows in moments of shared attention.

Chapter Fifteen

Moving On Together

Shayla and Juneau

Life rarely stands still for long.

After nearly three decades as a Senior Paralegal with the San Diego City Attorney's Office, mentoring staff and navigating complex cases alongside dedicated attorneys, I knew it was time to close one chapter and begin another. In June 2021, I retired.

The decision carried a swirl of emotions—pride in meaningful work completed, gratitude for friendships formed, and a quiet ache at leaving the familiar rhythm of my hometown. For the first time, I allowed myself to imagine a life beyond San Diego's ocean air.

Prescott, Arizona had captured our hearts during previous visits. Its small-town warmth, mountain air, and slower pace offered something different. Something inviting.

It felt a little like ziplining—stepping off a perfectly solid platform into open air, trusting the cable to carry you safely forward. Moving meant packing decades of memories into boxes, saying goodbye to what we knew, and stepping into a place where we knew no one.

The move required trust—not dramatic faith, just the willingness to step forward one day at a time.

So, in September 2021, we set our course for Prescott.

Our new home wasn't the sprawling ranch property I once imagined for a future dog rescue. But it came with unexpected gifts including a woodworking shop where George could finally pursue his long-held dream of becoming a professional woodworker.

This season of life unfolded more gently.

We found time—real time—to breathe, explore, and simply be present. Mornings carried the scent of pine along mountain trails. Afternoons brought leisurely walks around the historic courthouse square. On calm days, we kayaked across Goldwater Lake, sunlight dancing on the water's surface.

For a while, life felt spacious.

Training became a new shared focus with our dogs—not harsh, not rigid, but steady and consistent. Leadership grew quieter. Clearer. Shayla responded beautifully to that calm structure. She watched closely for cues, sometimes throwing herself dramatically into a "Down" with such enthusiasm that her belly hit the ground before the command was fully finished.

The more secure she felt, the more confidently she obeyed. The wild instinct and shepherd loyalty within her began to settle into balance. Eventually, she passed the testing to become an official American Kennel Club Canine Good Citizen—a milestone that felt especially meaningful for a former street survivor.

As obedience strengthened, so did our bond. We were no longer simply owners and pets. We were a pack connected by mutual trust and shared understanding. It took time to earn that trust, but in the process, we learned as much from Shayla as she did from us.

Of course, resisting rabbits remains an ongoing challenge.

Training Shayla reminded me of something travel has always taught which is you cannot control the terrain, only your footing.

By then, Shayla and Juneau walked beside me. They didn't pull ahead (except when I tell them to, great for uphill climbing), nor lag behind but instead remained attentive, and aligned.

I didn't yet realize how quickly life would shift again or how rescue, loss, and new beginnings would stretch our hearts in unexpected ways. But in that season, we moved forward together—steady, aware, open—trusting that whatever horizon lay ahead would unfold in its time.

Like the traveler who discovers that true connection comes not from sightseeing but from sitting still in a new land. Observing without judgment, trading stories, and calmly watching life unfold in a new way.

Chapter Sixteen

Bringing Tayen Home: A Blackhat Rescue

Tayen

The road to our dog Tayen began long before we ever heard of Blackhat Humane Society. It began the day Juneau died.

His sweet demeanor remained, but his legs trembled when he tried to stand and he would cry out in pain. The veterinarian told us there was nothing they could do to help. It was time to let go, like the closing of a well-loved book.

We laid him to rest on a soft blanket in a beautiful garden outside the vet clinic, surrounded by so much love and light. George knelt beside him, one hand resting gently on Juneau's back, I stroked the long hair on his soft paw. Shayla lay close, her face turned away, as though she knew his spirit was leaving us.

As he exhaled his final breath, a mist began to fall, delicate and quiet. We whispered, "Thank you" and "We love you always" to bless him on his final journey.

George whispered, "God reached out and took the brightest star from the sky to give us this dog."

We left rose petals and a family photo on his blanket, beside him. The drive home was silent. I glanced into the back seat at Shayla. She was still, her eyes misty, like tears. For the first time, she was alone. The star of "Shayla and Friends" now had no canine friend.

Our house felt so quiet. In the months that followed, Shayla changed. She was quieter, lethargic. She clung to us more, as though measuring the silence. Shayla waited at the door as if listening for a friend who would never return. Grief does not belong only to humans

Nearly a year passed.

The ache softened, but it did not disappear. And slowly, almost imperceptibly, the idea formed. Maybe it was time to open our hearts to welcome a new canine companion.

Not to replace Juneau.

I felt God changed our expected course with one more bend in the widening road, expanding our rescue journey.

That widening led us to Blackhat Humane Society (Blackhat), a small nonprofit serving the Navajo Nation in the Four Corners region (Arizona, Colorado, New Mexico, and Utah). There is no central shelter; they rely on a widespread community of volunteers, fosters, and quiet determination to rescue and heal.

On the reservation, stray dogs are everywhere. They are born beneath trailers, wandering near schools, surviving heat, cold, and hunger. Resources are scarce. Overpopulation is relentless. Without intervention, many simply disappear.

Blackhat steps into that space. Their volunteers travel miles of forgotten roads, saving one life at a time. They rescue. Vaccinate. Spay and neuter. Foster. Transport across state lines. They gently reacclimate the animals to life with humans, like mobile sanctuaries.

I so admire the Blackhat Humane Society volunteers and fosters. It takes a special kind of person to rescue and reacclimate animals with trauma, fear, and broken hearts.

In May 2024, a young shepherd-husky mix appeared on the Petfinder website as a Blackhat adoptable. They called him "Huskteen." Lanky. Silver-black coat with plumed tail. Alert eyes. Playful, good with dogs and people, the ad said. We saw his photo online and were interested in checking him out further.

I reached out and spoke with Toby, one of Blackhat's lead volunteers. She shared what information she knew about this dog, then connected us with his foster, Lavonne, who lived far north of Flagstaff. She texted additional information and pictures, but we were still so many miles apart. Logistics felt complicated. The distance was daunting. For a time, we hesitated.

We met other dogs in other shelters. Almost-right dogs. But my heart kept circling back to Huskteen as the "right" match.

Weeks later, Lavonne offered to drive him to Prescott. God must have smiled on this match made in heaven.

When we met him, that feeling only deepened. He was everything the photos had promised—silver-coated, bright-eyed, and full of life. He was cautious, untamed, carrying a wildness in his eyes. But we saw a softness beneath it. Just like Shayla. And his mannerisms and look reminded us so much of Juneau.

Shayla approached him with cautious curiosity. No growls. No tension. The moment we met him, just like with Shayla, we loved him. We were all happy to accept him into our home and family.

Lavonne and Toby later shared this dog's history with us. Before he had a foster, before he had a name, Tayen was a stray puppy in the remote town of Ganado, Arizona. Much like Shayla in Ukraine, he belonged with no one but survived on scraps of kindness—an occasional open hand or gentle voice. But at night he was truly alone. Not even a name. Strays like him usually weren't around long enough to truly matter to anyone.

One day, an Animal Control officer looped a catchpole around his neck and secured him in a metal cage on their truck. On the reservation, that often means the end.

But a maintenance worker saw what was happening and ran after the truck.

"Please," he pleaded. "You can't put him down. He's just a puppy. I'll take him."

The officer relented and handed the puppy over.

That single interruption altered everything. Although the worker could not provide a home, and the puppy moved through temporary care, uncertainty, even time tethered outside at a shelter in the elements, he was alive.

Then Lavonne met him and saw his gentle beauty. With Blackhat's support, she brought him home, socialized him, vaccinated him, prepared him for the life he might yet have.

The road led him to Shayla and us. From reservation stray dog to Shayla's companion, from survival to belonging, from one chapter ending to another quietly beginning.

We renamed him Tayen, a Navajo word meaning "new moon," or "new beginning." Named after the white wolf pup in my book "*Shayla & Friends: Into the Light.*"

He carried the alertness of a dog who had known uncertainty. In the first weeks, he darted through our front door and into the street, cars screeching as kind strangers thankfully stopped. Shayla chased him down and guided him home, as if reminding him: *This is where you belong now.*

She became the seasoned guardian, watching him vigilantly but patiently. Juneau would have been proud.

Tayen became her shadow.

One moment they are wrestling in the yard, tumbling in dust and sunlight, then collapsing side by side affectionately. Shared survival creates its own language. They understood one another without instruction. Perhaps it's the contrast between the memory of cold nights and empty bellies that makes a warm bed and a gentle hand feel like treasure.

Watching them, I realized something. Rescue is not simply about saving dogs. It is about refusing to let hardship have the final word. Grief narrowed our world. Rescue opened it.

With Shayla and Tayen together, our home and family feel complete again. In their companionship, a sense of sacred love restored, purpose renewed, seemed to fill our home, promising, "You are home."

Chapter Seventeen

Lessons in Love from Dogtree Pines

Nubbins & Tucker @ Dogtree

Dog lovers are not always content with just one or two dogs. Seems like our dynamic duo Shayla and now Tayen would be more than enough to keep our hearts full and our lives busy. But there's always room for one more, or sometimes 20+.

When people ask me how many dogs I have, I often smile and say, "Two and a half."

That always gets me a curious look and the inevitable question, "What's the half dog?"

I smile and reply, "He's a Great Pyrenees named Tucker."

Those familiar with the breed usually laugh and exclaim, "That's no half dog! It's practically a horse!"

True! But he just doesn't happen to live at my house. He lives at Dogtree Pines Senior Dog Sanctuary (Dogtree Pines). Although we didn't bring Tucker home to live with us, he found his own special place in my extended family as a dear friend.

I try to visit him a couple times monthly.

I began volunteering at Dogtree Pines a couple of years ago. What I didn't realize then was that I was walking into a classroom unlike any other. My teachers were gray-muzzled, wobbly, broken dogs, discarded by the world long before they reached this sanctuary.

They taught me patience, love, how to look beyond their scars to see the beauty in their hearts and forgiveness in the way they were still willing to trust people, despite what brought them to the shelter. And I've never been happier or more fulfilled. Although I had volunteered at prior animal rescues, this senior dog sanctuary is like none other.

Nestled among tall pines in Prescott, Dogtree Pines is a nonprofit sanctuary for senior and special-needs dogs. They are the ones most often overlooked. Gray muzzles. Clouded eyes. Arthritic steps. Much like the seniors I advocate for as an ombudsman. Some arrive with terminal diagnoses or a history of trauma. Others simply arrive unwanted, perhaps because of age or illness.

Here, they are neither forgotten nor discarded. They are honored, healed, and loved.

The compassionate founder Cindy Lamont and her devoted team are dedicated to helping seniors in need of medical attention, hospice care, and emotional support—whether for a peaceful transition or a joyful new chapter in their golden years. Their motto, "Dogs don't come here to die. They come here to live."

And live they do.

I have watched dogs once labeled unadoptable run through open fields months later. I've seen broken bodies respond to patient medical care, steady nutrition, and the kind of love that asks for nothing in return. A group of twenty plus dogs relating well as a pack. Some are adopted by families willing to embrace their final years. Others remain, held by fosters and volunteers who understand that dignity matters at every stage of life. They rediscover and share joy.

As Cindy states, "No dog deserves to die alone in a cage on a cold concrete floor, certainly not seniors that have given their entire lives to us."

My favorite, though I love them all, is my old friend Tucker. He is larger than life, a gentle giant. When he sees me, he ambles on over to me with that slow, deliberate grace unique to Great Pyrenees, leaning into our shared ritual. Sometimes I brush his thick white coat and talk to him for nearly an hour, his massive head resting in my lap, his breath deep and steady, snoring contently. Other times, we simply walk together beneath the whispering pines, his presence calming.

While most residents are seniors, a few younger dogs have found refuge here too.

Navi, once used as a bait dog in a dog-fighting ring, his body bearing the scars of past cruelty, is one of the few lucky ones saved. He is now free to chase tennis balls with wild joy.

Lady, a German Shepherd thrown into a canal, her back legs shattered. She learned to move again with the help of a custom walker and even skis in winter. She scooted through her final years with grace and grit.

Sweet Nubbins, thrown from a car, paralyzed and left for dead on the side of a highway, now runs and joyfully splashes in the lake. He is, without question, one of the gentlest, most loving souls I ever met.

Determined resilience and faith.

And shy Finn, another Great Pyrenees, still learning that hands can be kind and that love doesn't always leave. Watching him begin to trust is like witnessing a flower bloom in slow motion. He is learning to love our brushing routine too now.

Each dog carries a story. At Dogtree Pines, those stories are not erased. They are redeemed and loved.

Some of the dogs' rescue stories fill the pages of my book, *Shayla & Friends: Into the Light*. Each life, a lesson. Each moment, a reminder that healing is possible, even after the deepest wounds.

Watching these dogs heal, I can't help but wonder if God rescues us the same way—gathering what the world discards and calling it His beloved.

The road continues, sometimes through grief, sometimes through rescue, sometimes through quiet mornings beneath pine trees with a white dog leaning gently against my side.

And in those moments, brushing Tucker's coat while sunlight filters through the branches, I feel it again—that steady whisper of Spirit saying, "You are exactly where you need to be on this journey."

Perhaps you have felt it too somewhere along your own winding road. A pause. A bend in the trail where something or someone unexpected meets you and changes you.

We are all travelers of a sort.

Some of us walk with dogs at our side. Some carry loss. Some are still searching for the next horizon.

If you've ever paused long enough, you may have felt it too—that quiet reassurance that even the forgotten paths, even the detours, are guiding you home.

Chapter Eighteen

Into the Light - The Journey Continues

Now that Shayla is a certified Canine Good Citizen, I would like to train her as a therapy dog one day. She loves children so much, as if she remembers something about small hands and uncertain hearts. She endured tough times to emerge with a gift to share—offering comfort, resilience, and joy to others, both young and old. I imagine her gently connecting with children and teens who, like her, have known abandonment or adversity. One day when I retire as an Ombudsman perhaps she can sit beside me to comfort a senior. Even those who are simply shy or uncertain, like I was, can find strength in her steady presence.

So far, no therapy organization has welcomed a shepherd–wolfdog mix, even one raised among children. But I am not discouraged. Shayla would not give up, and neither will I.

Some callings take patience.

In the meantime, we dream of other adventures, and stories to be told. Hiking the open trails. Kayaking on Prescott's lakes. Shayla perched at the bow, ears forward, eyes scanning the horizon like the guardian she is, ready to jump into the sparkling water, living in the moment.

When I look at her, I see more than a dog. I see a tapestry of courage and kindness woven through many lives: the resilience of Ukraine, the faith of those who protected her, the wisdom of Juneau, the devotion of George, the compassion of friends across continents. She has walked through the darkness to find the light.

And now, wherever Shayla goes, she offers that light to others. She makes the world a softer, kinder place. So do Tayen and the rescue dogs. That's the beauty of dogs.

As I've reflected on her journey, I've wondered if the same might be true for us. The unexpected detours seemed to shape me. The crossings strengthened me. The companions, both human and canine, taught me how to trust again.

My story is proof that a closed door is often an invitation to a wider, more beautiful path than I could have imagined. Whether walking through the silence of a childless home, the grief of loss, or the disillusion of divorce, I learned that our purpose is not defined by what we lost, but by who we are becoming in His light.

Like Shayla and Tayen we are travelers who have come far. And even when the path bends through shadow, we are being led—sometimes quietly—to find the light in the darkness. We are never really lost; just waiting to be found.

Somewhere just ahead, there is a clearing in the forest pines, where the sunlight dances across the surface of a shimmering lake. I notice that even when I stop paddling my kayak and rest for a moment, a steady, invisible undercurrent steers me onward. I realize I am being guided all along, and I can just relax, not fight the current.

The same God who navigated a stray puppy to find what's across the ocean has been the current beneath my own boat, moving me forward even when I was too tired to row. He never left. I believe God does not abandon His travelers. Not the orphaned. Not the grieving. Not the weary. He rescues us because He loves us. He leads us to our forever home and family, just like Shayla.

Welcome home weary traveler. Follow God's light.

Shayla's Travel Journey

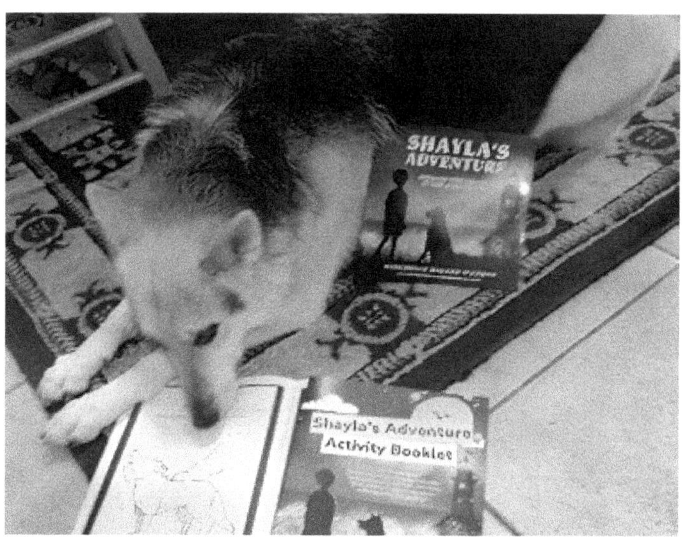

Chapter Nineteen
Epilogue: Faith Under Fire

Simba & Nala (The Saved & The Lost) – Father's House

We were so deeply touched by Roman and Bruce that we came to truly care about the people at Father's House and Ukraine, a country and culture so far away, one that we never knew about. It has been my honor to stay in touch with the Korniykos as friends. George, Shayla, and I enjoy visiting with Bruce and his wife Anne, about once a year on trips home to San Diego.

We followed the Korniyko family's journey as refugees to Germany when the war in Ukraine broke out, and to pray for their safety. They inspired me to tell their story, and Shayla's, to share their blessing and hopefully inspire others. Alina asked once, "Please don't let people forget us." Don't ever give up!

Early in 2022, Russian soldiers invaded Ukraine, eventually moving on to Kiev near Otchiy Dim. As news of the impending invasion became more real, Roman started preparing for the worst-case scenario. On the day the war broke out, though, all his plans seemed to fall apart. The buses he had planned on to evacuate the children and staff were all canceled. As he heard missile strikes all around their village of Petrivske, the staff moved the children to the bomb shelter. Roman's faith in God remained the only steadfast thing in his life. He prayed for protection and God provided a miracle.

He received a phone call from a Ukrainian stranger. The man said, "If you are ready in three hours, I will take your kids to the Ukrainian border."

The decision had to be made quickly. There was little time to weigh options.

With no time to spare, Roman obtained passports, readied a couple of minibuses on site, and mobilized the staff and children. They asked the children and adults not to eat anything as they would not be able to stop for the bathroom. Everyone, even the youngest children, understood and agreed, without crying or complaining. The man proved good on his word and arrived with two large buses, driving one of the buses himself. He even arranged for a police escort to the Polish border.

The orphanage's leaders, staff, and almost one hundred and fifty children (orphans and children of staff) were forced to quickly depart their beloved home that February night, taking just a few belongings and not knowing if or when they would return. Young children who had already lost so much through trauma, family betrayal, and abandonment, were now forced to move on again.

Police officers escorted the buses through crowded roads and highways, despite reports of the planned bombing.

Roman believes it was God's miracle they made it safely to Ukraine's border: "Angels guided us and made an open way for us."

When they were a few hours away from the border crossing, near Rivne, believing they were safe, the entourage stopped at a gas station so the kids could use the bathroom. Within five minutes of exiting the buses though, they started hearing constant bomb strikes and shelling all around them. Later they learned that it was the airstrikes bombing the Rivne airport. Their brave police officer escorts hid the children with their bodies, hands touching to provide cover over their heads as hovering angels as the kids ran to the bathroom and back to the buses.

With the kids safely back on board the buses, the police directed Roman and the bus drivers to turn off all lights, keep silent, and follow the officers at top speed through the dark night. The children lay on the floor, hands over their heads, not making a sound. The police escorts turned on their emergency lights and sirens to direct the buses where to go, focusing any shelling or bombing attention on themselves and away from the buses. Roman described these brave officers who risked their lives to protect the children as their angels, sent by God.

Once they reached the Polish border, the police returned to Ukraine. Before they left, they told the children not to be afraid or sad but to go with God: "Go in peace and come back in peace. Believe that with God's help we will do all we can to protect our Ukraine so that you can return to your home in peace."

In an interview, Roman said, "I saw God's hand in the officers who shielded the children, in the stranger who made the call, in the open border that night. "

He called their safe exodus a miracle. It took twelve hours to cross the border into Poland, but all were safe.

Days later, they arrived in Friedburg, Germany. A partnering non-profit of Father's House had made living arrangements for them. The community and even the town's Mayor welcomed the children, provided food and medical care as needed, and showed them to the initial shelter.

Roman initially had to leave his wife and daughters Alina and Anastasia behind at Father's House. The ladies stayed at the orphanage, with the two remaining dogs, a brother and sister pair of sweet Shepherds, Simba, and Nala. Sadly, the female dog Nala strayed away from home and, despite Alina and Anastasia's days of search, was never found. Hopefully, she joined the stray animals still in Ukraine, rescued by animal organizations and good citizens.

After a couple of weeks, the women were able to leave, with the remaining dog Simba, and safely drive to the border. They reunited with Roman and the children, and Simba was adopted by a loving forever family in Germany.

Roman spoke of how difficult it was to be refugees in a new land where they must depend on others, and to leave their ministry, home, and beloved country. He speaks of those days with quiet conviction. He sees God's hand woven through the details.

He once stated, "Compared to Russia, Ukraine is such a small country, but David was also small and he was victorious over Goliath because God was with David. I want Ukraine to trust not in its strength, but to trust in the strength of God. Ukraine will stand and we will return home."

Currently, the remainder of Roman's under-age orphans now live safely in Germany. What was meant to be temporary shelter became long-term. New systems, new authorities, and new family arrangements reshaped their future.

Bruce Elliott and the Ambassadors of Father's House (the United States liaison for Father's House) continue to support this orphanage. Bruce's work with "Ezra International" is involved with child rescue in other countries; the Ezra Mobile Child Rescue Unit and partnering with the "Life at 100%" rehabilitation house for mothers and children in Ukraine.

The Korniyko family has returned to operate Otchiy Dim in Ukraine. We are uncertain of Mykola's current status.

Meanwhile, back at Otchiy Dim, some of the male staff have joined the Ukrainian army, fighting for their beloved homeland. In the past couple of years, team leaders focused on wartime operations and education: creating bomb shelters and reinforcing the buildings, when necessary.

Following the current events of Ukraine, and Father's House in particular, reminds us that we are all united in spirit through God's love. As casualties continue to rise, churches are destroyed, statistics increase on the billions of dollars of infrastructure damage, innocent people and pets killed in the streets, children kidnapped and taken out of Ukraine; it sometimes seems so difficult to keep faith in God.

Yet, as Roman said, "Ukraine will stand and the people will return to their beloved homeland." Till then, we join Roman and the brave Ukrainian people with our prayers for peace.

Bruce has informed me that unfortunately, America's Center for Disease Control (CDC) has now banned future dog rescues from Ukraine. Fortunately, Shayla came to America when she did.

Staying connected to them has deepened my understanding of what faith looks like under pressure. It is not loud. It is not polished. It is steady. I could not have imagined how intertwined our story would remain with Father's House. I see now that what began with a single rescue dog was never only about one dog.

The mission of Father's House now is to preserve life and serve as many children and adults as possible by sharing God's love, through both word and action. Under the leadership of Anastasia and Alina, Father's House has become a refuge for families wounded by war. Through *Restored Life*, mothers, and children in distress (widowed, orphaned, homeless due to war and domestic abuse) rebuild stability. Children who missed years of schooling receive tutoring and encouragement. Fathers House was licensed to run its own school. Young adults without parental support are mentored through *Step Into Life*, learning practical skills for independent futures. Offering educational and rehabilitation programs and psychosocial support.

Their thrift store still serves the community. Renovations continue on the future coffee shop where the barista school, teaching youth job skills, will reopen. Even in uncertainty, seeds are being planted.

Father's House was never just a building in Ukraine. It was and is a light. A place where children of all ages learned they were seen, chosen, and loved.

I continue to pray for peace over a land that first gave us Shayla.

The story is not finished. It never really is.

But through every chapter whether it be rescue, relocation, or rebuilding, I have seen enough to trust that we are never walking alone. God who was in the story from the beginning is still in the story now. The journey is not over. It is still unfolding. May we continue to walk in courage, in compassion, and in prayer, out of the darkness and into the Light.

Shayla's Song - ***Shayla's Here ...***

Shayla's here

Little ones

Freedom's near

Just begun

Just around the corner from this

Love is waiting in your midst

The day has dawned

A brighter one

A greater life has just begun

Hope anew

Will unfold

Perfect love

From the bold

Time to cast all fear away

Step into a better brighter day

Traveling across the sea

Adventure waits for you and me

Shayla's here

Gift of God

Miracle

From the Lord

Music and Lyrics Cassie Bedore; Vocals Lauren Bedore; Arrangement
Barry Bedore©
Available on the website:

Acknowledgments

My heartfelt thanks to the Korniyko family, Mykola, Bruce, and Anne Elliott for sharing your journey—and Shayla's—with me, and for entrusting us to be her forever home.

To my husband, George: your steady encouragement made this book possible. Thank you for embracing my love for dogs through muddy paws, dog hair, and all the joyful chaos that completes our family.

I am forever grateful to my parents, Herbert, and Shirlee Bolger, who taught me a deep love for animals and gave me a stable, loving childhood home. Their example shaped the compassion that guides my life to be a voice for the voiceless. And to my brothers - those by blood and by heart, especially Buzz - for your guidance and friendship.

To my creative team: my marketing coach, Tracy Glass, for helping me understand why this story matters; and my editor, Leslie Rager, for her hard work and dedication. To my wonderful friends and readers — thank you for teaching, supporting, encouraging, and believing in me, even when I sometimes doubted myself. I'm grateful to walk this journey with you as friends and fellow dog enthusiasts.

I honor my sweet Shayla and all of my incredible pet companions — Tayen, Juneau, Riley, Honey, Blaze, and Misty—who taught me patience, acceptance, gratitude, courage, faith, and genuine love. And to my "other" dogs, Tucker, Nubbins, Boltan, thank you for showing me true friendship and trust.

Most of all, I thank God for inspiring this story and blessing my life journey with these extraordinary human and canine friends. Your love has been faithful, even when my dogs remember Your teachings better than I do.

Author's Bio

Barchelle ("Chelly") **Bolger Wathen** is a spirited storyteller, animal advocate, and retired senior paralegal from San Diego, now living in Prescott, Arizona. With a Master of Public Administration, she continues her commitment to public service as a State Ombudsman Specialist and volunteers with local dog rescues.

Her writing reflects her journey, shaped by resilience, compassion, and faith, inspired by the redemptive bond of animal companionship.

She loves exploring God's creation, spending her time kayaking, ziplining, and hiking mountain trails with Shayla and Tayen.

Chelly is the author of *Shayla & Friends*, the true story of her wolfdog mix's journey from a Ukrainian orphanage to her home in America; the *Shayla's Adventure* children's series; and the young adult novel *Shayla & Friends: Into the Light*, all celebrating courage, faith, friendship, redemption, and the transformative power of rescue.

Other Works by the Author

Please continue to follow Shayla and Friends (Teen/YA & adult) and Shayla's Adventure (children's series) at:

Instagram: https://www.instagram.com/juneaushayla/

Website: https://www.shaylaandfriends.com

Newsletter sign up & email: info@shaylaandfriends.com

SHAYLA & FRIENDS: INTO THE LIGHT (Teen/YA; also eBook)

SHAYLA'S ADVENTURE: FINDING THE LIGHT IN THE DARKNESS (Midgrade children)

SHAYLA'S ADVENTURE ACTIVITY BOOKLET (All children ages)

SHAYLA'S ADVENTURE: WHAT'S ACROSS THE OCEAN?
(Young children) (forerunner to Finding the Light in the Darkness)

SHAYLA'S ADVENTURE: HOME FOR CHRISTMAS (Seasonal young kids picture book)

Giving Page

A portion of sales proceeds from all Shayla books benefits the following charities:

Ambassadors of Father's House (AFH) (501(c)(3) U.S.-based support for Otchiy Dim/Father's House orphanage in Ukraine (https://www.facebook.com/ambassadorsoffh/about)

Blackhat Humane Society (501(c)(3))
(https://www.blackhathumanesociety.org/)

Dogtree Pines Senior Dog Sanctuary (501(c)(3)) (https://dogtree pines.com/)

References

America, T. C. (n.d.). Retrieved from: https://czechoslovakianvlcak.org/#team-7

Club, A. K. (n.d.). Czechoslovakian Vlcak Dog Breed Information - American Kennel Club (akc.org). Retrieved from https://www.akc.org/dog-breeds/czechoslovakian-vlcak